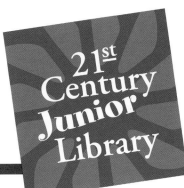

21st Century Junior Library

RESPECT

by Lucia Raatma

CHERRY LAKE PUBLISHING * ANN ARBOR, MICHIGAN

CHERRY LAKE
Publishing

Published in the United States of America by Cherry Lake Publishing
Ann Arbor, Michigan
www.cherrylakepublishing.com

Reading Consultant: Cecilia Minden-Cupp, PhD, Literacy Consultant

Photo Credits: Page 4, ©JUPITERIMAGES/Creatas/Alamy; page 6, © iStockphoto.com/aabejon;
cover and pages 8 and 18, Jupiter Images/Brand X Pictures; page 10, © Rob Marmion, used under
license from Shutterstock, Inc.; page 12, © Karen Struthers, used under license from Shutterstock, Inc.;
cover and pages 14 and 20, © Monkey Business Images, used under license from Shutterstock, Inc.;
cover and page 16, © Kruchankova Maya, used under license from Shutterstock, Inc.

LIBRARY OF CONGRESS CATALOGING-IN-PUBLICATION DATA
Raatma, Lucia.
 Respect / by Lucia Raatma
    p. cm.—(Character education)
 Includes index.
 ISBN-13: 978-1-60279-320-0
 ISBN-10: 1-60279-320-4
 1. Respect—Juvenile literature. I. Title. II. Series.
 BJ1533.R4R33 2009
 177'.1—dc22   2008030560

Cherry Lake Publishing would like to acknowledge the work of
The Partnership for 21st Century Skills.
Please visit www.21stcenturyskills.org for more information.

CONTENTS

Talking in the library can bother people who are trying to read.

What Is Respect?

Hayley and Rachel were at the library. They were waiting to check out books.

"Can you come to my birthday party next Friday?" asked Hayley.

"Yes, I can't wait!" Rachel replied. Then she noticed people frowning at them.

"Let's talk about it outside,"she whispered. "We're not being very respectful. People can't study while we're talking."

Respectful people do not tease or make
fun of others.

Respect is treating others the way you would like to be treated. It also means thinking about other people's feelings. You don't show respect when you **insult** or make fun of others.

Respectful people are polite. They listen to other people. They get to know people before making **judgments** about them.

Think!

Remember a time when someone was rude to you or teased you. How did it make you feel? Would you ever want to make someone else feel that way?

Do you think this boy is showing respect
for his sister?

Showing Respect

There are many ways to show respect. At home, listen to your parents. Be kind to your brothers and sisters. You are not showing respect when you tease them.

Be respectful of other people's things. Ask before taking or borrowing something. Be careful not to break things that belong to other people.

Show respect for your teacher by listening
carefully to her lessons.

At school, you can show respect by not hurting others. Calling people names is not respectful. Everyone has feelings. It is important to remember how others might feel.

You can also show respect by listening to your teachers. Their advice will help you learn more and stay safe.

Create!

Make a list of people you respect and look up to. It might include parents, teachers, or others who have helped you. Share the list with your parents or an adult you trust. Talk about why you respect the people on the list.

Take turns and follow the rules when playing games with friends. This will show your friends that you respect them.

You can show respect for your friends. Be patient and take turns when playing games. Help friends learn how to play the games that you like. Be willing to try new games that your friends like to play.

You can also show respect by listening to a friend who has a problem. When you listen to others, you show that you respect their feelings.

Learning about a friend's culture shows your respect. It can also be fun!

Respecting Your World

It is important to treat everyone with respect. When you meet new people, try not to judge them. Sometimes people feel uneasy around other people who are different. Take the time to learn about new people, **cultures**, or ideas.

Showing respect may be as simple as playing with a younger neighbor.

You can show respect in your neighborhood by treating others well. You should never play tricks on your neighbors. Damaging other people's homes or yards is not showing respect.

Instead, you can offer to help a neighbor with yard work. Or you can play with a young neighbor whose mom is busy. They will both be happy you helped!

Recycling is an easy way to show
respect for Earth.

Another way to be respectful is to take care of the **environment**. You show respect by not littering or wasting water. You show respect by **recycling** bottles, cans, and paper. Choose to keep Earth healthy. Your efforts will **benefit** people now. You will also be helping keep Earth clean for future people!

You will feel good when you show respect for others. They will be happy, too!

When you show respect, your friendships with other people can become stronger. Your family will know that you care about them. The way you treat others can make a difference in their lives. They will treat you with respect, too!

Look!

Watch the people around you. Notice how your neighbors talk to one another. See how kids you know treat their friends. Do they show respect? How could they be more respectful? Share your ideas with your parents or friends.

GLOSSARY

benefit (BEN-uh-fit) to be useful or helpful to someone or something

cultures (KUHL-churz) the ideas, customs, and traditions of different groups of people

environment (en-VYE-ruhn-muhnt) the world around you, including the land, sea, and air

insult (in-SUHLT) to say or do something rude or upsetting to others

judgments (JUHJ-muhnts) opinions about someone or something

recycling (ree-SYE-kling) processing old items so they can be used to make new products

FIND OUT MORE

BOOKS

Kroll, Virginia L. *Ryan Respects*. Morton Grove, IL: Albert Whitman & Company, 2006.

Suen, Anastasia. *Show Some Respect*. Edina, MN: Magic Wagon, 2008.

WEB SITES

Respect—A Way of Life

www.cyh.sa.gov.au/HealthTopics/ HealthTopicDetailsKids.aspx?p=335 &np=287&id=2356
Read more about respecting yourself and others

Whootie Owl's Stories to Grow By

www.storiestogrowby.com/choose. php
Find folktales and fairy tales about respect and other good character traits

INDEX

ABOUT THE AUTHOR

Lucia Raatma has written dozens of books for young readers. They are about famous people, historical events, ways to stay safe, and other topics. She lives in Florida's Tampa Bay area with her husband and their two children.